I must
'BE-ABOUT'
my Father's business!
© Copyright 2008 Daniele Luciano Moskal

ISBN 0-9545113-2-8

Published By Unique Writing Publications

Unique
WRITING PUBLICATIONS

To

Faye, Rebecca, Carla, and Kazzy

Author's Note

I am eternally grateful for the divine supernatural revelation of the Holy Spirit who birthed this Children's **'BE-ABOUTS'** ministry within me in 1999. Without God's special grace and inspiration this project could never have been completed.

THANK YOU MY LORD AND MY GOD!!

For me the most enthralling part of writing this book has been the chance to retell this profound and astoundingly unique, touching, memorable, true story of Jesus' first words spoken and found in the Holy Bible in the Gospel of St. Luke, chapter 2, and verse 49, in an easy-to-comprehend way to the children of this world, that brings it within the scope of a child's own emotions and experience. I hope I have succeeded, and to whatever extent I have, the chief debt of gratitude must go to the Holy Bible (God's infallible Word), itself for preserving such a rich heritage of material I can use to teach the **'BE-ABOUTS' Generation**, with wisdom, understanding, and above all simplicity that children of, say, seven years of age and upwards will be able to understand Jesus' remarkable childhood without great difficulty. I dedicate this book to my greatest encourager for his agape love, patience, enthusiasm, inspiration and aspiration, – my best friend, the Holy Spirit – I LOVE YOU!!

To and all the millions of "Be-Abouts" through out the four corners of the earth who have been blessed by my ministry – DANIELE LOVES YOU ALL IN JESUS CHRIST'S LOVING NAME – **Amen & Amen!!**

Many centuries ago, the country of Judah in Israel was under the rule of the Roman Empire who had conquered it again. The Romans called it Judea and it remained a separate kingdom, ruled by a Jewish king named King Herod. All though Herod ruled Judea, the real power, however was really in the hands of the Roman governor, Pontius Pilate. During King Herod's reign a God-fearing priest also lived in the land of Judea whose name was Zacharias. Both he and his wife Elizabeth loved God and obeyed His commandments, but they were sad because Elizabeth was childless and of old age.

"Oh God of Abraham, Jacob and Isaac, give us a son", they continuously prayed. One day Zacharias was taking part in a holy service in the Temple at Jerusalem when an angel of the LORD appeared to him.

"Do not be afraid, Zacharias", the angel spoke. "God has heard your prayer. You and your wife Elizabeth will have a son and you will call him John. He will be a great teacher and a man of God. He will be filled with the spirit of the prophet Elijah; he will bring the people back to God and prepare the way for the coming of our LORD."

"How can this be?" Zacharias asked.

"I and my wife are too old to have a son."

"I am Gabriel, the messenger of God", the angel replied, "and God has sent me to you to deliver this message. But because you have doubted His Word you will be struck dumb and you will remain like this until the things I have told you shall come to pass."

When Zacharias left the Temple and arrived at his home, he could not tell his wife Elizabeth about the angel's visitation because he was struck dumb. But Elizabeth told him:

"We are going to have a child. God has arranged it – for He has heard our prayers!"

Now a few months after the angel Gabriel had visited Zacharias and Elizabeth, God sent the angel Gabriel to a small town called Nazareth in Galilee, to visit a young Jewish peasant girl called Mary. She had been promised in marriage to a carpenter named Joseph, who was descended from the family lineage of King David of Israel. The angel appeared to her and said unto her:

"Greetings, Mary, You are highly favoured and God's blessing is on you."

When Mary saw the angel and heard what he said she was filled with wonder and felt uneasy. "Mary, do not be afraid", the angel reassured her.

"God loves you; He has filled you with His grace. You will give birth to a child, a son whom you will call Jesus *(YESHUA)*. He will be great, and people will call Him the Son of the Most High God. God will give Him the throne of His forefather King David, and He will reign over Israel forever.

His kingdom will be an everlasting kingdom and it will never cease to exist."

"But how can this be so?" asked Mary.

"I have never slept with any man."

The angel Gabriel replied, "The Holy Spirit of God is with you; God will over-power you. And because of this, the child born from your womb will be called the Son of the Most High God."

The angel then began to tell Mary about the supernatural miracle God had already done for her cousin Elizabeth.

"Through God's will your cousin Elizabeth will also have a son. And you know Mary that she could not have children before because she was barren and seemed to be much too old to bear any now, but she will give birth before you. With God everything is made possible."

Mary then replied:

"Behold I am God's servant. May everything come to pass just as you have said it?"

It wasn't several months passed by when Mary rushed to visit her cousin Elizabeth, who was staying in a town in the hills. When

Elizabeth saw her coming in the distance she was suddenly filled with the Spirit of God. She quickly ran to welcome Mary and they embraced each other.

"You are highly blessed and favoured among women", Elizabeth told her cousin, "and so is your child! You are the mother of our LORD, and you have filled my house with light. Why, when you greeted me just now, my own child suddenly leaped for joy inside me! How important it is for a woman to believe in God, for you and I are living proof that He can perform supernatural miracles!"

It wasn't long after Mary had visited her cousin that a son was born to Elizabeth. As of the Jewish laws, when the baby boy was just eight days old he was taken to the Temple to be circumcised , which was – and still is to this day – the custom of the Jews, and to be named.

The people who where gathered at the Temple believed the boy would be called Zacharias, after his father. But Zacharias could not speak, except by using signs, but he remembered the angel Gabriel's words. So the people brought him a slate and he wrote on it:

"His name shall be called JOHN!"

As soon as he wrote these words down, Zacharias' mouth was loosened to speak again and he cried out:

"Praise be to God! This child John will be a prophet of the LORD who will free us, and deliver us from all our enemies. He will go ahead to prepare the way for the LORD who shall come. He will tell the people that their sins are forgiven and that they shall be saved. Then God in His mercy and love will send us a light. It will shine on everyone who feels lonely and fearful, or lost or frightened of dying, and the light will guide us all towards everlasting peace!"

Spring passed to summer, and summer passed into autumn, and the baby Mary was carrying slept in her and began to grow. By the time winter came Mary's body was heavy and full, for it was time for her child to be born. During this time Judea was part of the Roman Empire and everyone in the province including Mary and Joseph had to obey the laws of Rome.

The Roman Emperor Augustus issued a proclamation that every man and woman who lived in the lands had to pay taxes and register themselves and their children. So a new register was drawn up, by which every citizen name would be records of the people's place of their birth. King Herod heard this command and ordered everyone in his kingdom to return to their place of birth to be put on the register. Because Joseph belonged to the family of David, he had to leave Nazareth where he lived and worked as a carpenter, and go back to Bethlehem, which was approximately some 70 miles to the South. Joseph's wife Mary had to go too, even though her child was about to be born. Together they set off with their mule over the hills to Bethlehem. They arrived in the city at evening time, and tried to find somewhere to stay but the streets were crowded with people coming from the hills and valleys to be registered. Every where Joseph went to find a place for them to rest he was turned away by the landlords. The night was falling fast, and Joseph wrapped his cloak around Mary and led her, and the mule she was sitting astride on down the street. Joseph kept knocking at the door of other houses, hoping for a room for the night or a place to rest their heads. One woman opened her front door only to shout at the top of her voice that there was no room, and rudely shut the door in their faces. Mary slipped gently off the mule, because she was tired and it was near time for her child to be born.

They walked on further until they came to an inn. Lamps were burning in every window and the rooms inside were full of people eating and drinking. Horses, camels and donkeys stood munching their food in the courtyard. Joseph knocked on the door. The landlord opened it and shouted to them.

"No room at the inn!", and waved then away.

As they moved on the light from the door fell on Mary.

"You can sleep in the stable just a little further up the road, if you like. There is plenty of fresh straw," the landlord called after seeing Mary was with child and about to give birth any moment. Mary and Joseph thanked the kind inn-keeper and there, inside the stable with an ox and the donkey beside her, she gave birth to her son. She wrapped him up in a swaddling cloth and laid him in a manger filled with fresh straw. She called him

Jesus, which means, "God saves".

That very night the words of the prophet Isaiah came true:

"For unto us a child is born; unto us a son is given; and the government shall be upon his shoulders, and his name shall be Wonderful, Counsellor, the Mighty God, and the Everlasting Father".

In the hills surrounding Bethlehem shepherds were out in the fields, taking care of their sheep flocks during the night. Suddenly an angel of the Lord appeared to them, and the glory of God shone all around them. The shepherds were terrified because of the great light that shone so brightly.

"Don't be afraid," the angel reassured them. "I have good news for you this evening – tonight in the city of David – a Saviour has been born in Bethlehem. His name is Christ, the LORD!"

Then the light shone brightly so that its splendour lit up the fields as if it was daytime, and the sky was filled with hundreds of angels of God. Their voices rose like the wind and swept over the hills and valleys as they sang in unison:

"Glory be to God in the highest, and peace on earth and good will to all men!"

Then the light and the chorus of angels gradually faded away and the shepherds said to one another.

"Let us go quickly to Bethlehem and see the holy thing that has happened there!"

They ran down into the town and found the stable where Mary and Joseph were resting. They saw the baby sleeping in the manger, and kneeled down and worshipped it. Then they went out and began to tell all the people of Bethlehem what had happened, and everyone was amazed. Mary treasured all these memories and often thought about them as Jesus grew up.

The people of Judea didn't realise that a star had risen over Bethlehem. They didn't even notice that the nights were no longer dark, that a new star, brighter than any other star had suddenly appeared in the sky directly above the stable where Jesus had been born. King Herod heard for himself of the star through three strangers – wise men came to visit him from the East. "What is that great light that has appeared over your country?" they asked.

"We have noticed a new star in heaven. It doesn't seem to move like the other stars, but seems to stay fixed in a place above one particular spot in Judea". Herod looked at the wise men. They were old, and obviously skilled at the understanding and interpreting the movements of stars and their meanings. But somehow Herod could not understand what the wise men were talking about. Their next question took him by surprise.

"Where is the new child who is born to be the king of the Jews?" they asked.

"What did you say, a king!!?" he shouted out.

"Yes, a king of the Jews, we believe he is the Messiah, the Saviour that the whole world is waiting for. That is why we have come along way to pay homage to him that is why we are here now."

Herod was very angry he did not like the idea of another king that would take his place. He called for his learned scholars and wise priests, and asked them.

"What do you know about a new king to be born here in Judea? Is it true we are to have a Messiah?"

"Yes, my lord, it is true. The old writings of

the prophets of old say so," the priests and scholars replied.

"When and where? , the king demanded. One of the old scholars stepped forward.

"It's all written down in the book of the prophet Micah, my lord", he said.

"It's to happen in Bethlehem. This is how Micah the prophet wrote it down but the meaning is clear – 'and thou Bethlehem, in the land of Judah, art thou not the least among the princes of Judah: for out of thee shall come a Government that shall rule my people Israel.'"

Herod had heard enough and immediately

turned to the three strangers and shouted in a rage.

"Find me this so-called king of the Jews, and return back to me and tell me where he is, for I want to go and worship him too!!

But Herod was lying; he wanted to kill the child because he didn't want any threat to his throne while he was yet governor of Judea.

The wise men set out once again to follow the star which shone even more brilliantly than before in the eastern sky. The light drew them onwards, and they followed it all the way to Bethlehem where it seemed to stand still.

There they found Mary and Joseph, and the baby Jesus, lying asleep in the hay. They now knew that this was the new king they had travelled so far to find, and they bowed down on their knees and worshipped him. Then each man reached into their own saddlebags attached to their camels and drew out their special gifts to present to the child they had brought with them. Gently they laid their gifts in the hay around the child as Mary and Joseph watched in awe.

One of the three wise men gave gold, which represented a gift and a sign for kings. The other gave frankincense which was used to burn on the altar of God; this was to represent a priest. And the last one gave myrrh, which was used in those days to help preserve men's bodies after death.

In Jerusalem lived an old man called Simeon who prayed on a daily basis for the coming of the promised Messiah. "Please, God, "He prayed, "Let me see just once the Messiah, then I shall be able to die in peace."

God told him, "go to the Temple, and there you will find him."

That same day Mary and Joseph had taken Jesus to the Temple as was the custom of all Jews to present back to God their first born son as a thanksgiving. She and Joseph also offered a pair of turtle doves to God. Simeon waited patiently outside the Temple and when he heard the cry of the child as Mary walked past him his heart quickly skipped a beat and he knew that this was the promise that God had spoken to him and all of Israel were expecting. He went in to the Temple and spoke to Mary these words: "Blessed be God," and gently took the baby from her and raised the child to the heavens and whispered these words to God:

"Lord, now your servant can die in peace, for his prayer has been heard. My eyes have seen the salvation that will come to all men. The light that now shines on earth will bring glory to your people Israel."

Then he turned to Mary, who was standing amazed at the words Simeon spoke, and spoke these words as he gave the baby back into her arms:

"Your child will make many men great, and will cause some to fall. But there will be people who will not believe in him, and a

sword shall pierce your heart with sorrow."

When Mary and Joseph had finished making

their offering to God, they went back to

Bethlehem with their child Jesus.

I must

'BE-ABOUT'

my Father's business!

(Scripture reference from the book of Luke 2:49)

In the Book of **Luke chapter 2 and verse 41**

tells us that every year, Mary and Joseph

"went to Jerusalem for the Feast of the

Passover." At the age of 12, Jesus accompanied Mary and Joseph—the only incident of his youth recorded in the Gospels. At 13 he became a "bar mitzvah" (son of commandment) and from then on he was considered an adult, allowed to read the *Torah* in the synagogue and to ask questions about it. The year preceding this age, devout Jewish families were obligated to acquaint their sons for the religious obligations of adulthood, one of them being a pilgrimage to the Holy City. Deuteronomy 16:16-17 named three festivals that required pilgrimages to the

Temple in Jerusalem: Passover *(Pesach)*, Pentecost *(Shavuot)* and Tabernacles *(Sukkoth)*. Distance prevented many from attending all three, but most Jews tried to make Passover. This obligation fell to all males, who were commanded not to appear empty-handed: "Each of you must bring a gift in proportion to the way the Lord your God has blessed you." (Deuteronomy 16:17) Furthermore, because of concerns for safety on the road, it was customary for Galileans to travel in large groups. When Jesus was twelve years old he went with his Jewish parents to

Jerusalem. It was their habit to make a pilgrimage there every year to give thanks to God at the feast of the Passover. He joined in offering the sacrifice of a lamb (free from blemish and spot), honey and wine, and ate the crisp, hard, unleavened bread that reminded the Jews of their flight from Egypt.

After the festival was over his parents set out to go back home to Nazareth.

"Where is Jesus?" Mary asked.

"He must have gone ahead with the other pilgrims", she was told.

But when they looked for Jesus among the crowds of pilgrims they could not find him anywhere. Deeply worried, Mary and Joseph hurried back to Jerusalem. They spent three whole days looking for Jesus in all the bazaars and market-places in the city, and asking if anyone had seen a boy who looked lost but they could not find him. Then someone said that they saw a young boy who resembled Jesus in the temple. Being their last hope, Mary and Joseph hurriedly went into the Temple, to see if he was there.

"There he is, look, in Solomon's Porch!" cried

Joseph. Jesus was sitting among the scholars who taught in the Temple, as if he were one of them. He was asking them all kinds of questions and listening attentively to all their answers, and everyone who heard him teach was amazed at his wisdom.

"My son, what are you doing?" Mary cried. "We have been so worried about you!"

Calmly and gently Jesus replied, "Why did you look for me? Didn't you know that I would **'BE-ABOUT'**, my Father's business?"

Then he went back with them to Nazareth. As

Jesus grew older, he learned to become a carpenter just like Joseph. But it was obvious that God, His Father had given him special wisdom and grace, and everyone who knew him loved him.

I must
'BE-ABOUT'
my Father's business!

© 2008 Daniele Luciano Moskal

I must
'BE-ABOUT'
my Father's business!

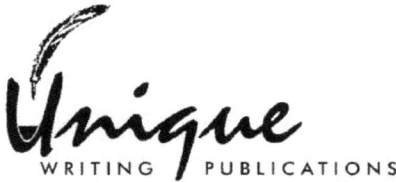

I must
'BE-ABOUT'
my Father's business!

© 2008 Daniele Luciano Moskal

www.ingramcontent.com/pod-product-compliance
Lightning Source LLC
Chambersburg PA
CBHW060651030426
42337CB00017B/2560